Long Division

poems by

m.nicole.r.wildhood

Finishing Line Press
Georgetown, Kentucky

Long Division

Copyright © 2017 by m.nicole.r.wildhood
ISBN 978-1-63534-298-7 First Edition
All rights reserved under International and Pan-American Copyright Conventions.
No part of this book may be reproduced in any manner whatsoever without written permission from the publisher, except in the case of brief quotations embodied in critical articles and reviews.

ACKNOWLEDGMENTS

A version of *Preparing for Family Gatherings* was published by *Red-Flag Poetry Service* under the title *Vapor*.

Wang's Chinese Diner,1990; No Dinosaurs Before Bed; Post-Its; How to Use Water as Fuel (under the title *Feud Fuel*) and *Maybe Rivers* were published by *Five Magazine*.

Publisher: Leah Maines

Editor: Christen Kincaid

Cover Art: Mark Wildhood

Author Photo: Mark Wildhood

Printed in the USA on acid-free paper.
Order online: www.finishinglinepress.com
also available on amazon.com

Author inquiries and mail orders:
Finishing Line Press
P. O. Box 1626
Georgetown, Kentucky 40324
U. S. A.

Table of Contents

Evaporation 1

My Parents' Second Child 2

Wang's Chinese Diner, 1990...3

No Dinosaurs Before Bed 4

Young For Now 6

This is Just a Drill..7

Post-Its 8

Cementation...9

Is It That I Didn't Stand Up for You?..................................10

Sharing the Back Seat...11

Grounds for Growing Up 12

Standing Where We Played 13

How to Use Water as Fuel..14

Long Division..15

The Letter From My Sister...16

Preparing for Family Gatherings..19

Maybe Hope...20

Let Us Be Light..21

Maybe Rivers...22

Growing Up Is "Goodbye" by Another Name 23

A Dead, Dead Rose 24

for my family, of origin and chosen

Evaporation

Sun burns like judgment,
even in its soft peek down,
giving away its diamonds to the sea.
Sea doesn't know that this is for free
so it parses and parts with small

enough pieces of itself to scale
the wavy cords of light.
Now each—the many beaded bodies of water
and the bright twines linking and lifting them—
know what it is to come completely apart in union.

My Parents' Second Child

The castles in every detail around me: Lake
Washington's moving mask of wavy blue

below the great crowd of clouds playing chess,
all of God's flowers being published

under bilingual rain that vacillates
between slender streaks and sweaty sleet.

There is enough light for all my apartment's
windows. There are not enough windows.

Are there pictures of her and I on walls
opposite *her* windows for the Ohio sun to fade?

We see each other in person once a year now.
She mutters her navy disdain for me

in our family dinners and holiday games
tradition forces us to replay

with and for each other, the rest of our clan
that sees of itself what it has always seen—

we can speak many languages—hate, fun, apathy—
but we do not know who among us understands which.

Wang's Chinese Diner, 1990

I was told: this was your first
time eating out
you were an extrovert
but we didn't know until then.

I remember: faint lights
swaying on barbless wire
conversation throbbing
like a distant ocean.

"Hi, we're the Johnson[1] family," I said
to the waitress. "This is Mom,
Dad and *our* baby Jamie."
I was on the table by the time—

I remember: the table,
did they get it so round
by rolling it down a hill
over and over?—

"our baby Jamie" got introduced
to everyone. I was told: you stood
on the table, pointing
at her pale face, her eyes closed

in thin, perfect arcs, like far-off
birds. I remember she looked
made of porcelain. I remember
her igneous eyes when they opened

at the plunk of dinner plates in front
of us. I remember never being told
she was not meant to replace me.
I was told: we love you, over and over.

---

[1] Names throughout the collection have been changed.

No Dinosaurs Before Bed

On my Saturdays, we are skipping—
I demanded, after a warm-up round of Hopscotch—
to the fairgrounds an hour before they open. I ask:
What does Jamie do on her Saturdays?

She gets one a month, I get one a month
while Mom stays at home with our new brother.
It's special time with Dad, and it's a way to give
me and Jamie a break from each other. Our bed

in the room we share takes up most of the space—
we each get a skinny area of carpet next to our side for toys.
Mine are in plastic mesh baskets until she takes out my
T-Rex and Longneck and Stegosaurus for her dolls to ride.

That's probably happening right now, as Dad turns coins
into candy, cotton and all else. Dad snags a bouquet of balloons
that nod along to the carousel's music where I get to ride
life-size versions of My Little Ponies.

Jamie only got five Daddy Saturdays because Dad signed her up
for a wood-fairy-princess take on Girl Scouts.
They were gone every Thursday night and a weekend
every other month. My Saturdays: endless; fair days

until the fair didn't come back. A face painter
worked up a sunset on my forehead the year they set
him up next to a paleontologist whose midlife crisis revised
her passions. She now made milky chocolate molds of any

prehistoric creature you wanted. I asked for Finn. Finn?
The name of her Stegosaurus, Dad would have to explain.
I couldn't have a bite till after dinner. I asked.
When my sister graduated from the princess program,

long after the fair dispersed, I asked if that meant
she had become a queen. I asked how she became a princess.

She asked if I thought you could teach something like that.
I asked if she knew how much longer we'd be sharing

a room and plucked one of her Disney Princesses
off of Finn by its hair. I whirred it slowly over
my head until it slipped away from me, the shine on its dress
making it too stiff to billow and slow its fall.

Jamie seized Finn by his tail and slung him out our window
as the Princess arced, head first, cleanly into her nose. She rushed
both hands up to her face and cried and cried. We only had to share
a room for five more months, but we had to move before I could find Finn.

Young For Now

"They don't know humans, so they are fearless."
~William Vollman[2]

They, the girls, braid each other's hair, slide on sandals
and grab thin, purple jackets they won't need for the summer outside.

Below a furious drum of sun in skinny clouds,
color-drained weeds faint like discarded bits of sewing thread.

The stream is still trying, drooling down the hills to the heat-packed
stables. The horses are having more difficult births.

All the adults comment on how hot everything is,
how everything is beaten with heat. How neglected they feel by rain.

When Uncle Joe, heat-worn, comes looking for help
with the harvest, the girls take their books and run by the brook

and sit, feeding the mosquitos. The world is a sea of flesh.
They giggle and squirm, till the younger one jumps up, runs to the water,

grabs the rope, swings across. The other eyes the current,
stays on shore, braces while her sister pendulums

over frigid stream and fills the moment with glee.
Who will be in trouble if the rope, the moment, breaks?

They forget about their books, though reading is a required
bodily function, run home at the first spot of dark.

They do not yet see the shortage of ponies.
They do not know they need to say goodbye.

So they don't. The world is open sea,
but not enough leagues will flush the need.

---

[2]Harper's Magazine, March 2015.

This is Just a Drill

really bad Mexican food
and skeeball tournaments
at *Casa Bonita* in Denver

an enormous adobe house
outside pink and turquoise
inside furious with festivity

synchronized swimmers
cave divers haunted house
gift shop arcade robots on tightropes

a family tradition to visit
when the Boston cousins come
to Colorado in the summer

youngest of the them
Lauren, age four,
wanders off one visit

the rest of us in the queue
like at airport security holding
our gummy, green food trays

a giant red noise
opaquely white light flashes
the ceiling opens up

fire sprinklers coating all patrons
sister clutches my hand—maybe
the last time—holds on until even after

we find Lauren holding open the fire exit
looking up and around, confused
the only one to stay dry

Post-Its

Ages:
    nine and three-quarters (me);
    six (Jamie).

Tools:
    electric screwdriver from Dad's shop;
    hammer *(Ibid)*;
    the kitchen scissors;
    by the end, four snapped spoons.

Results:
    a passageway through drywall, storm-gray plaster
    connecting our two closets
    waiting—
        centuries in my Toy Horse kingdom;
        her dolls would grow up to have families of their own—
    for the sister whisper
    or the flashlight's blink in sister code

    or toilet-paper roll with yellow, sticky-back message:
        what we had for lunch
        my advice for her future self
        a sketch of what our future dog might look like

    a hole I never could fill

Cementation

A saturated sky fell apart over our pasture:
snow's big reach gathered us all like a mama hen
for those five eventides before the strong-armed storm
gentled back to our usual terse wind and endogenous wet

that bears us so much. We broke fruit for the first time
that year much later than usual, then continued to
note the peace or distress of each parcel
of land, placing bets, hopes, for next season.

Next season brought Caterpillars and men in yellow
with personal stop signs to burn
their tar ribbons through our uneven fields,
their machines stumbling as they blunted our harvests.

We swatted at black dust. We coughed into cupped hands
or paisley bandanas. We held vigil for the buried bugs and
blades of grass, kneeling with our mother beside the husks—
insect, crop, meadow.

Is It That I Didn't Stand Up for You?

I'm the kid who watched
the kid who teased
the kid who took longer
than the rest of the kids

to stop sucking her thumb
learn how to lace her shoes
let go of Mom's hand
stop fearing the playground swings

and, in becoming an adult, when
I was told by other adults that evil,
to root and metastasize, only needs
the darkness of good people's silence,

I ran back to that little girl's room
in our parents' house to find the curtains
tied like a girl's pony tail
and all the windows closed and dim.

Sharing the Back Seat

George got the middle row of our new 1996 minivan,
which looked like the egg of a terrifyingly huge
bird, all to himself. Dad pulled over just before
Durango to flip the backseat backwards
so you and I would stop picking
on our little brother. I thought we were going
to see the blue knife that fashioned
the Grand Canyon, holding up the atlas
up to my tinted window, which Dad had cracked a little
to circulate air, trying to get the inside (map)
to match the outside (wild).

The sky was flecked with fowl and barely able
to contain the bloated heat. Slender threads of water
reflected blue until we got to get out and run off
some energy somewhere near Mesa Verde.
You were the first to plunge into the water's
tawny belly, but my toes were the first to turn
as blue as the streams looked from the car.
You cupped some of this transparent toy,
rough with sandy hitchhikers from its slow descent

into stone, in your hands, and tossed it
in my face. From that close, it wasn't
blue or tan. It was clear. The plan wasn't
ever to go to the Grand Canyon. Mom spread
green-striped towels over the seats and we
continued, you and I, riding backward until
the land swallowed up all those feeding flumes
for birds, to where we could be in four states at once.
We passed so many signs that we could only see
the backs of, so I never did find us on my map.

Grounds for Growing Up

Roses together, Dad coaxes,
folds hands as if to pray.
We dig with the same thin hands
through separate bags of seeds,

folding hands as if to pray.
We're young but already want
separate species of seeds.
We look up at Dad, whose smile we have.

We're young but already want
the same rows for different plants.
We look up at Dad, whose smile we have
but are not using.

The same rows for different plants—
Mom and Dad plotted all of this for us, we see
but are not using
roses together, like Dad coaxes.

Standing Where We Played

Tule Lake, across the street from Nana and Pop's house,
has broken many plates of sun, swallowed many sunken,

emergency-red plastic boats and been force-fed a bike path's
worth of stones that mostly failed to skip.

Sullenly—I'm 15—supervising siblings and cousins,
I know the adults think I know when to intervene

(squash the fun), when to let the cousins yell at each other,
or my sister at me, when to let ships sail.

Each wave knows when to rest, when to rebel;
all the more if it's slit in half or impaled clean through.

I, age 9, age 15, age 21, age 27, now, still halt at every upturned little hull—
on Tule Lake's coastline or elsewhere—drying in the mist-busting sun.

How to Use Water as Fuel

Dad says I should have been born a fish,
what with the eerily natural way I moved through water.

He and I got our scuba diving certificates
together when I was 12—I didn't notice

the Caribbean makes your hair sticky as it's drying
under a sun I didn't care would rudely

find every last fleck of flesh exposed.
My sister rejected diving, getting in the water

at all, because of what the wild does
to your hair and skin.

We glossed arguments in the family,
like makeup on my sister's face. I had to be

persuaded to start wearing the stuff because it seemed
like both Mom and sister needed a cleanup crew

every night just for their faces. They used water
to wash; I used it to fly.

Long Division

It has been years since any calls, any letters,
and now over two since the latest wedding—
hers. I solicited the sky not to rain on her trip
down the grassy aisle with our parents;
ask it now how it makes distance keen with beauty.

We are the ones who move. From all the way inside
the same person to intervaled naps and playground
bruises on fledgling bodies. We learned the same
language from the same people.

And we filled our shared room up with it till it poured
into the sky, which would hold all our curses and nightly prayers;
soon, our dead. Maybe she no longer stirs while she should sleep;
I'm awake at night for different reasons now.

When I do sleep, my hands still lose feeling, feel like they swell.
It's not my two-year-old sister clinging tightly to my arm
in our screeching floral bed to get through terror-gobbled nights.
That stopped even before we both grew all the way up,

became afraid of different things (though I still the dark
and admit now to miss the tiny bruises from a protect-me cling), moved.
Time has hollowed out our grandfathers. But she and I and the lack of 'we'
soak in the sameness of repetition—we have made distance our habit,

let its arms maim our ties. Lots of time makes things settled.
Time gives us all it has every day and we use this staggering
giving-all of the self to excuse letting more slip by like more
is guaranteed on the way, to still not move.

The Letter From My Sister

"I once wrote a poem about us—*Broken Sisters*.
I thought we'd always be that way. Hostile, hurting."[3]

> She's nineteen. I'm twenty-three, reading this in Dublin
> on a solo summer tour of Western Europe and the UK.

"Fighting. I didn't understand you. I thought you judged me.
I thought you were pessimistic, self-destructive."

> I've asked seventeen friends, family members and professors
> to write to me about me. I was surprised my sister responded.

"I wondered what you had against me. You were angry, took it
out on those who care the most. I vowed never to be like that."

> I didn't know her—what I did know, I didn't understand.
> It was more than being different people, our clashes.

"We're different, but we're sisters, and we're a lot the same.
We're both very thoughtful and love to dance and write."

> I took pride on being different from her, always following
> the rules, never experimenting with alcohol, obeying curfew.

"You were a free spirit. Danced to the beat of your own drum.
You did your own thing, didn't show it if you cared

what other people thought. I thought you maybe didn't care
enough what other people thought."

> It took me two anguished months to finalize my list
> of people to ask to write me letters.

"Asking us to write these letters to you, knowing that not
everyone has nice things to say, shows me

just how much you've changed. You do know you're not perfect and you are using that to guide you to yourself. To grow."

> Hers was the second letter I read; neither one had been
> the compass I'd hoped for in collecting these letters.

"And not be angry that not everyone likes you
and everything about you all the time.

It's hard being the oldest; the parents were stricter on you than me,
I know things were different for us, but I always wondered

why you didn't see what I saw. You were always dissatisfied,
unappreciative. Always wanted more. Are you still like that?"

> When I asked people to write letters, I gave only two
> specific requirements. One: be honest.

"I learned from you, though. You'd get mad when Mom said you
couldn't go somewhere; she'd tell me *you catch more bees with honey*

than vinegar. I learned to be nice and gain their trust.
Parents are a lot easier to work with when they trust you.

It's one thing to have expectations. All we want, though,
is for you to be happy for more than just fleeting moments."

> And two: I'm not looking for advice as much
> as encouragement. Don't give advice.

"Easier said than done, but I know you will find a way.
It's a journey, not a destination. Enjoy the ride

even when you're dissatisfied. If you were happy all
the time, it wouldn't be special or as worth it.

We're opposite in a lot of ways, but we grow more alike
as time passes. We both overthink things, for better or worse."

In the journal I'd bought in Belfast for reflecting on these letters, I write: *does she know this is advice?*

"Just remember not to forget to actually live life; don't let your overanalyzing ruin the enjoyment of the moment.

Your imperfections make you who you are and you should be proud of that."

And: *we're different, but we're sisters, and we're a lot the same.*

---

[3] The material in quotation marks is an adaptation of what my sister actually wrote in a letter to me in 2009.

Preparing for Family Gatherings

Try, if you can, to think yourself a cloud.
I write.

*It may help: we are not so very
different from them:*

*Clouds move along with more ease and often
see more light.*

*But we are both full of nearly nothing,
both have our fits,*

*our accolades. Neither of us knows when
to keep our shadows*

*or how to stay still in wind or avoid getting
blanched by sun.*

I stick the note on the bathroom mirror, end it:
even the commonest of us can tremble with light.

Maybe Hope

The slip of the sea
taut between the lip of launch
and the kiss of finish;
the frightened days ending summer,

still buoyant with boundless light
but crouching into smaller and smaller spaces;
each dawn as it bloats.
We are all waiting to be whole.

Sun is a wholehearted giving of self,
unending even as the moon alone makes
any effort at mutuality.
Creation does everything for fullness.

This is what the stem and the bird
and the claw and the clasp
and the den and river-sawed canyon
and wager of seeds are.

Let Us Be Light

In our stone coats, our hearts plunging-blue in us,
we walked the same courses—school, home, the mall.

Training turned instinct. All bodies of water
are manmade where we grew up.

They swell hospitably after a big snow,
as if swallowing the spate of sun.

When I come back to Colorado to visit,
the millpond in the horse pasture next to our otherwise

suburban high school—we weren't ever students
there at the same time—seems to cower under

its top hat of ice as if it's fighting off the light.
Maybe my sister and I should be more like the pond.

We can only stand on the sifting silt of parallel shores
and feel the thrill between our toes—me trying to grasp

all the grains—as God is tipping the quaking bottle
of creation and, thumb in its punt, pouring it all all the way out.

Maybe Rivers

A quiet congress of taxed Colorado water-
courses has my answers, I'm hoping.
They're full in my memory—there they
still go to the same places—the bulbs of bushes
tracing them green as grief.
The next visit home, I ask for the keys
to my parents' 4Runner, drive to the Platt and find it
now trout-less, filled only with self-doubt.

The Highline Canal, by my childhood house:
now a mere crack in the earth lined with brittle leaves
and snow so dry it might be Styrofoam.
Is it me that's deaf and blind, or is it the past?
She and I could not really have played here,
in sticky summer, chased chipmunks
or skipped rocks from one side far to the other.
My sister and I couldn't have

tied jump ropes to the petrified Aspen branches
and slid messages in a tin bean can
from her all the way to me and back
over snow glazed over like a bored kid's eyes.
I see no trace of our leaves-and-mud forts
that lasted through fierce winters. The Aspens' arms
have grown closer together, the houses, also, and
even the canal's sides, too.

Growing Up Is "Goodbye" by Another Name

Wait for dark (moon: "I'll show *you*
simmering light), push out.
You won't spot the shore.
Grief is the thwart.

The night. It has no bottom.
It is the bottom.
Light will thwart when it comes again.
The shore will seem longer than life.

Submerged and raveling at the edges, too.
(Rumi, rose,) How can celebration be
falling apart when sky and sea
are blue come together?

A Dead, Dead Rose

There is too much room inside these horrid florid metaphors. They are holey, strung out like an old sock looking for its partner, lost
after the blunt-toothed cave of reeling heat.

m.nicole.r.wildhood is a freelance writer who grew up in a small suburb of Denver, Colorado and moved to Seattle when she was 20 years old after being the first in her family to drop out of college. When she did finish, she received a Bachelor of Arts in theology from Seattle Pacific University. Her blog, meganwildhood.com discusses politics, poverty, mental health and disability, with a particular focus on the unsustainability of the pursuit of individualism. She aspires to create a body of work that advocates for and itself emanates social and ecological justice.

m.nicole.r.wildhood's poetry, fiction and short nonfiction have appeared in *The Atlantic, The Atticus Review, a great weather for MEDIA anthology* and other anthologies, as well as *The Sun, Ballard: A Journal of Street Poetry* and *Forage Poetry,* among others. She was a finalist for *America Magazine's* annual *Foley Poetry Contest* and received a Top-25 honorable mention in *Glimmer Train's* annual short fiction contest, both in 2016.

She has been a registered scuba diver and saxophone player for over half of her life; both of these interests have afforded her the opportunity to travel. A particularly memorable trip, she was selected as a rising high-school senior for a national honor band and got to tour Western Europe performing in Frankfurt, Paris, Vienna, Luxembourg and other cities. She currently writes for Seattle's street newspaper *Real Change* and is at work on a novel, short stories and several poetry projects, including one in Spanish.

www.ingramcontent.com/pod-product-compliance
Lightning Source LLC
LaVergne TN
LVHW041519070426
835507LV00012B/1687